SQUADRONS!

No. 71

The Curtiss
KITTYHAWK

- The Canadians -

Phil H. LISTEMANN

ISBN: 978-2494471-26-9

Copyright

© 2024 Philedition - Phil Listemann

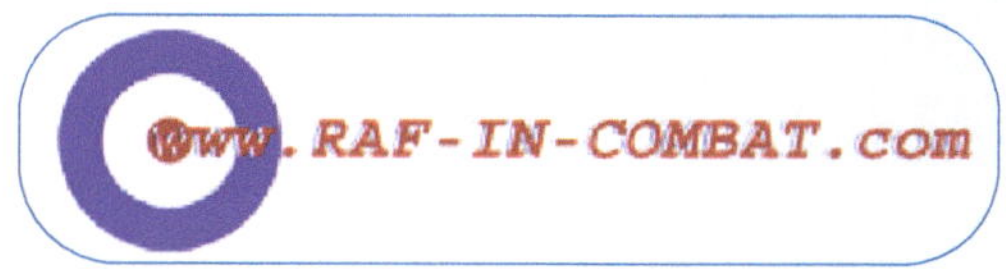

Colour profiles: Gaetan Marie/Bravo Bravo Aviation

GLOSSARY OF TERMS

PERSONEL :
(AUS)/RAF: Australian serving in the RAF
(BEL)/RAF: Belgian serving in the RAF
(CAN)/RAF: Canadian serving in the RAF
(CZ)/RAF: Czechoslovak serving in the RAF
(NFL)/RAF: Newfoundlander serving in the RAF
(NL)/RAF: Dutch serving in the RAF
(NZ)/RAF: New Zealander serving in the RAF
(POL)/RAF: Pole serving in the RAF
(RHO)/RAF: Rhodesian serving in the RAF
(SA)/RAF: South African serving in the RAF
(US)/RAF - RCAF : American serving in the RAF or RCAF

RANKS
G/C : Group Captain
W/C : Wing Commander
S/L : Squadron Leader
F/L : Flight Lieutenant
F/O : Flying Officer
P/O : Pilot Officer
W/O : Warrant Officer
F/Sgt : Flight Sergeant
Sgt : Sergeant
Cpl : Corporal
LAC : Leading Aircraftman

OTHER
ATA: Air Transport Auxiliary
CO : Commander
DFC : Distinguished Flying Cross
DFM : Distinguished Flying Medal
DSO : Distinguished Service Order
Eva. : Evaded
ORB : Operational Record Book
OTU : Operational Training Unit
PoW : Prisoner of War
PAF: Polish Air Force
RAF : Royal Air Force
RAAF : Royal Australian Air Force
RCAF : Royal Canadian Air Force
RNZAF : Royal New Zealand Air Force
SAAF : South African Air Force
s/d: Shot down
Sqn : Squadron
† : Killed

CODENAMES - OFFENSIVE OPERATIONS - FIGHTER COMMAND

CIRCUS:
Bombers heavily escorted by fighters, the purpose being to bring enemy fighters into combat.

RAMROD:
Bombers escorted by fighters, the primary aim being to destroy a target.

RANGER:
Large formation freelance intrusion over enemy territory with aim of wearing down enemy fighters.

RHUBARD:
Freelance fighter sortie against targets of opportunity.

RODEO:
A fighter sweep without bombers.

SWEEP:
An offensive flight by fighters designed to draw up and clear the enemy from the sky.

The Curtiss P-40 Kittyhawk

Called the Warhawk in American service, the Curtiss P-40 was the most numerous fighter type on hand when the United States entered the war in December 1941. A development of the Curtiss P-36, the P-40 was essentially a P-36 equipped with an inline Allison V12 V-1710. The French were the first to express an interest in this model, known as the H-81, having already ordered the export version of the P-36 (the H-75). The H-81 would later be purchased by the USAAC and the RAF (as the Tomahawk). Curtiss continued to improve the breed and a new production model, the H-87, was soon available with a new version of the V-1710 that had a spur-gear reduction mechanism, raising the engine thrust line. This caused the nose profile to be redesigned, hence the new designation.

The RAF became interested in purchasing this version (as the Kittyhawk). They were destined for use in the Middle East to replace the Tomahawks already in service there. At the time, in 1941, the British aviation industry was at full capacity and unable to supply the required number of fighter aircraft for all fronts (including the Far East which needed reinforcement with the Japanese threat increasing). Hurricanes could be supplied for overseas operations, but their numbers were not enough so they had to be backed up by American-produced types. Based on the P-40D/E, the Kittyhawk Mk.I/IA was used in large numbers (over 750) until the British ordered the next model, the Kittyhawk Mk.II, which was based on the P-40F and L models powered by a Merlin engine. The Kittyhawk Mk.III was based on the P-40K and M models, which reverted to the Allison engine, as did the Kittyhawk Mk.IV (P-40N), the last version produced. The design did not see any major improvements between 1941 and 1944; the P-40 could not compete with newer types introduced to other air forces. Obsolete as a pure fighter by 1943, it remained a good fighter-bomber and flew effectively in this role until the end of the war, even though it was steadily being replaced.

WITH THE RCAF

The Royal Canadian Air Force (RCAF), wanting to reinforce its defensive fighter force, initially considered licenced production of the Bell P-39 Airacobra. That never came to fruition and the project was abandoned due to the unavailability of engines. Consequently, an agreement was reached with Britain and 72 Kittyhawk Mk.Is (P-40Es) bought by the British Purchasing

Kittyhawk AK571, the first Kittyhawk Mk I for the RAF. The very first few had a four 0.50-in guns in the wings like the P-40D.

The last RCAF model was the P-40N or Kittyhawk Mk IV. Being the final production model, the P-40N featured a stretched rear fuselage to counter the torque of the more powerful, late-war Allison engine, and the rear deck of the cockpit behind the pilot was cut down at a moderate slant to improve rearward visibility.

Commission were diverted to Canada. All were extracted from the AK571–AL230 batch and were taken on charge by the RCAF between October 1941 and January 1942. These aircraft flew with their RAF serials until June 1943 when they received the RCAF sequence **1028–1099**. Even aircraft already lost in service received an RCAF serial but, of course, these were never taken up. This batch was followed by 12 Kittyhawk Mk.IAs diverted from a Lend-Lease contract for the RAF (ET serial range) in April 1942. In June 1943, they received the RCAF serials **720–731** (also covering aircraft already written off). In January and February 1943, to make up for attrition, Canada was directly given a batch of 15 Lend-Lease P-40Ms, which retained their USAAF serials before receiving **831–845** in June. This batch was almost immediately followed by the delivery of 35 P-40Ns between May 1943 and September 1944. Their RCAF serials, **846–880**, were allocated in relatively short order. Of the 134 Kittyhawks taken on charge by the RCAF, 75 survived the war.

Furthermore, when deployed in Alaska, the RCAF borrowed nine P-40K-1s from the USAAF in November 1942; the survivors were returned to the Americans in June 1943. In all, eight RCAF fighter squadrons were equipped with the Kittyhawk, all in Canada. It was also the only RCAF fighter type to engage the Japanese in the Aleutians as two units, Nos. 14 and 111 Squadrons, on rotation, served under American command in the area. When Canada was called to help the Americans in Alaska, two wings were formed to control the RCAF's light bomber and fighter units. X Wing, formed on 2 June 1942 and employed on air defence and anti-shipping duties, was disbanded on 15 September 1943 following the withdrawal of the Japanese from the Aleutians. On 14 June 1942, Y Wing was also formed at Annette Island and employed on defensive duties. It was disbanded on 18 November 1943, when the squadrons were redeployed to Prince Rupert, having seen little operational activity in the meantime.

Victories - confirmed or probable claims: -

First operational sortie:
06.06.42
Last operational sortie:
21.11.43

Number of sorties: *ca.*225

Total aircraft written-off: 6

Aircraft lost on operations: 2
Aircraft lost in accidents: 4

Squadron code letters:
YA, *none*

COMMANDING OFFICERS

S/L Blair D. RUSSEL	CAN./ C.1319	RCAF	02.01.42	27.11.42
S/L Bradley R. WALKER	CAN./ J.3205	RCAF	27.11.42	...

SQUADRON USAGE

Authorised to be formed within the Home War establishment on 2 January 1942, 14's formation was immediately initiated at Rockliffe (Ottawa) and command given to F/L (later S/L) BD Russel, a Battle of Britain veteran with No. 1 Squadron RCAF (see *SQUADRONS! No. 26*). The first aircraft to arrive were North American Harvards on the 10th. It was only at the end of the month that notification was received explaining the squadron would be equipped with 15 Kittyhawks. The first fighters arrived soon after and acceptance tests were carried out. On 4 February, while on one such flight, the CO experienced an engine failure, owing to a lack of fuel pressure on AK983, and was obliged to make a forced landing on a frozen river, fortunately without serious damage. A few days later, F/L LV Fayle damaged his Kittyhawk (AK950) overshooting the runway. A third incident occurred on the 22nd with AK952, and two more followed on the last day of the month. At the end of March, the squadron moved to Sea Island in British Columbia where it would stay for almost a year. In the next few weeks, while no major incidents occurred, the daily serviceability rate remained low with the number of Kittyhawks fluctuating between five and ten (of the 15 aircraft on charge). The situation became worse as the number on hand reduced to just 11 in August following several accidents. From that point, serviceability improved markedly, reaching an operational standard, and would be maintained. Also, the number of Kittyhawks had increased to 14 by the end of the year. So far, the squadron had only suffered minor accidents, with no one injured. This changed on 2 October when P/O Arnold Ridgway was killed in the crash of AK952 on the north shore at North Vancouver. It appeared he lost control while attempting to fly out of overcast. At the end of November, S/L BR Walker assumed command from S/L Russel. During the year, little operational flying was carried out and the situation remained the same during the first weeks of 1943 until the squadron moved to Alaska on 11 February to reinforce the Americans. As the weather in the region is rather bad at this time of year, the squadron took its time to complete the move to Alaska, finally arriving at Elmendorf Field on 1 March (to join X Wing two days later). Soon after the unit's arrival, the Americans asked the Canadians to change the roundels on the aircraft, but this was hindered by a lack of paint. Over the next few days, the Canadians continued their trip to Umnak in the Aleutians. Some uneventful defensive patrols of the aerodrome and the vicinity were carried out on the 27th (2) and the 28th (4). However, on 28 March, 14 recorded its first loss in the region when P/O JW Tomlinson, who had joined the squadron the previous month, was killed on the aerodrome when he crashed in AK851. On 31 March, 12 pilots departed by air transport for Adak. On 1 April, another accident resulted in the death of Sgt HG Anderson in AK982. Anderson had also joined the squadron in February and was still on training on the type. Two weeks later, AK914 was also damaged in an accident but without major consequences for the pilot, F/O JG Housego.

The squadron's baptism of fire occurred on 18 April. That day, S/L Walker led three other pilots – F/L DW Wakeling, F/O JA Grimmins and F/O AW Roseland – on a dive-bombing operation to Kiska Harbor, which they completed without incident even though the sporadic flak was accurate. The next day, the Canadians participated in a mission with the USAAF's 11th and 18th Fighter Squadrons. That day, they worked in pairs. After a couple of days without sorties, the Canadians returned to the Japanese targets around Kiska three times on the 26th. The three dive-bombing efforts represented a total of 22 sorties carried out without incident. On the 30th, the weather near the target prevented completion of the job and the eight pilots, led by the CO, were obliged to return. It was hoped to postpone the strike for later in the day, but it never happened. In the evening, four Kittyhawks scrambled to intercept an unidentified aircraft

Bradley Reardon WALKER
Can./ J.3205

Enlisting in the RCAF in May 1940, Walker was trained in Canada and graduated with a commission in November. Posted overseas, he joined No. 2 Squadron the following month, a unit which became No. 402 (RCAF) Squadron in March 1941. In December 1941, he was given a flight commander's position with No. 403 (RCAF) Squadron, which he held until September 1942 when he was rested with a DFC awarded in June. Repatriated, he was given command of No. 14 Squadron RCAF in November for service in the Aleutians. He accompanied the squadron to England where the squadron became No. 442 (RCAF) Squadron in February 1944. Walker left 442 at the end of April and was repatriated in July. No further operational positions followed before he left the service in May 1945.

Curtiss Kittyhawk Mk I AK893
No. 14 Squadron, RCAF
Umnak, Alaska (USA), summer 1943

which proved to be an American Catalina. In all, the squadron flew 52 sorties in April. On 1 May, two dive-bombing attacks were flown, both in the morning, and were considered successful; the Canadians were congratulated by the intelligence officer. In the afternoon, the squadron was not on the roster, but four pilots were loaned to the 18th Fighter Squadron as they were short of pilots. Flying Officer McDuff and Sgt AE Clarke went on their first trip and Flight Sergeants NH Hobbie and JP Jessee on their second. The next day, the Americans still having personnel issues, four Canadians were loaned. On the 3rd, the squadron patrolled all day from 6.00 to 22.00 hrs while two pilots completed a sortie with the Americans. The squadron returned to dive-bombing duties on the 4th and destroyed a Japanese flak installation while another handful of sorties was completed by the pilots attached to the 18th Fighter Squadron. These were actually the final sorties carried out by 14 for the month but some the unit's pilots flew operations with the Americans on the 6th. The same day, Wing Commander REE Morrow, the X Wing CO, had to bale out of 42-9205 while on a local patrol with an American pilot. They had taken off downwind and trouble began right away. The canopy of Morrow's P-40K started to roll open as it had not been locked shut. Being downwind, the cockpit immediately filled with dust and it was at that moment Morrow made a mistake; he took his hand off the throttle to close the hood. By that time, he was well down the short strip but not at flying speed. He tried to correct but was too late. He struck a bank and drove his undercarriage through his wing root. The aircraft began to stall because the propeller had been bent in the collision and could not deliver enough power. Morrow managed to gain altitude, but the vibration was so bad he was left with no choice but to abandon the aircraft. He landed safely in the cold water, managed to climb into his dinghy and paddled to shore in about 35 minutes, meeting some soldiers who had waded into the water. They carried him into a tent. Sadly, Morrow's hip had struck the tailplane as he baled out and the resulting vertebral fracture would require over two months of recovery. In June, defensive tasks were assigned to 14. During the month, the squadron had four Kittyhawks on readiness from one hour before sunrise until one hour after sunset. This arrangement was activated twice, on 4 and 5 June, but the few scrambles undertaken were uneventful. Otherwise, the tasking comprised dusk and dawn patrols; operational hours for June almost reached 100 hours as a result. No operational activity was recorded between 1 and 21 July and the unit had to wait until the 22nd for something to happen. That day, a dive-bombing op was carried out by seven aircraft. The dive was initiated from 13,000 feet and the bombs dropped between 6,500 and 6,000 feet. Three fell in the water. Two days later, 14 completed a new kind of attack, high-level bombing. They followed up with three more raids the next day, two on the 26th and a single one on the 27th.

At the end of July, eight more Kittyhawks and ten pilots were transferred from No. 111 Squadron. This move was supervised by W/C Morrow, who had recently returned from his recuperation. On 14 August, Kittyhawk 1099 was seen crashing into the Bering Sea about 15 miles east of No. 1 Satellite. Pilot Officer RM Bell, an American from Arkansas, was posted missing on a local patrol. His wingman, P/O WR Campbell stated he saw Bell diving into the sea at about a 70-degree angle from about 500 feet. Three weeks later, the squadron lost another pilot when P/O Rodney Shavalier, in 1093, crashed near the cloud-covered peak of Mt. Idak.

In the meantime, the RCAF flight at Amchitka continued its operations. The Canadians were also active in August with six operations: dive bombing on the 3rd and 12th (twice), reconnaissance and strafing sorties on the 10th and 11th (twice) and a reconnaissance by two Kittyhawks on the 11th. No more sorties were scheduled as the island was thought to have been deserted by the Japanese; this was later confirmed. The presence of the Canadians therefore became unnecessary, so X Wing disbanded. The move home was undertaken from 21 September and 14 was back in British Columbia at Boundary Bay on 6 October. The squadron immediately began preparations for a move overseas; it had been earmarked to be sent to the UK and incorporated into the 2nd Tactical Air Force where it was renumbered No. 442 (RCAF) Squadron (see *SQUADRONS! No. 52*).

Kittyhawk AL218 wearing 'YA' codes. Previously, this aircraft was briefly used by No. 111 Squadron RCAF. The codes were discontinued from October 1942. Reserialled 1093 in June 1943, it was lost in September with its pilot, P/O R Shavalier.

A Kittyhawk of No. 14 Squadron RCAF, with the codes 'YA-P', at Sea Island in July 1942. The serial is not visible.
A line-up of Kittyhawks at Umnak in Alaska early in the summer of 1943. The aircraft identified are AK893/B and AL144/O.

Some pilots of No. 14 Squadron during the Alaskan summer of 1943.
Left to right: Pilot Officers G.G. Millar (†28.09.44 with 442 Sqn), W.L. Pigden, H.C. Morse, S.V. Garside (†07.06.44 with 440 Sqn), W.D. Peacock (†04.05.44 with 440 Sqn), and W.R. Campbell (†01.08.44 with 442 Sqn).
Crouching: W/O C.O.R. Clacken and P/O J.H. Clarke. With the exception of Millar and Campbell, all were posted or attached from No. 111 Squadron on temporary duty in July 1943.

F/L A Grimmins, recently returned from five weeks of flying with American pursuit squadrons in missions over Kiska, briefs P/O A.C. Fanning, F/O W. MacLean, P/O K. Barrie, P/O R. Cox, F/O G. Stiles, F/O F. Galbraith, F/Sgt H. Hobbie and F/Sgt R; Bell (USA, †14.08.43).

Date	Pilot	S/N	Origin	Serial	Code	Fate
06.05.43	W/C Robert E.E. **Morrow**	Can./ C.1238	RCAF	**42-9205** [1]		-
14.08.43	P/O Raymond M. **Bell**	Can./ J.27371	(us)/RCAF	**1099**		†

Total: 2

[1] *Borrowed from the USAAF.*

Date	Pilot	S/N	Origin	Serial	Code	Fate
02.10.42	P/O Arnold **Ridgway**	Can./ J.13996	RCAF	**AK952**		†
01.04.43	Sgt Harold G. **Anderson**	Can./ R.86274	RCAF	**AK982**		†
15.04.43	F/O James G. **Housego**	Can./ J.11971	RCAF	**AK914**		-
06.09.43	P/O Rodney **Shavalier**	Can./ J.27824	RCAF	**1093**		†

Total: 4

Kittyhawk AK987/T under maintenance with a simple canvas cover to protect the engine during the summer of 1943. The tough conditions the groundcrew worked in to maintain the Kittyhawks is evident. This aircraft, later reserialled 1066, returned to Canada and served until the end of the war with various RCAF units.

Victories - confirmed or probable claims: 1.0

Number of sorties: *ca.***600**

First operational sortie:
01.07.42
Last operational sortie:
12.11.43

Total aircraft written-off: 11

Aircraft lost on operations: -
Aircraft lost in accidents: 11

Squadron code letters:
TM, LZ, *none*

COMMANDING OFFICERS

S/L Arthur D. NESBITT	CAN./ C.1327	RCAF	03.11.41	12.06.42
S/L John W. KERWIN (†)	CAN./ C.922	RCAF	12.06.42	16.07.42
S/L Kenneth A. BOOMER	CAN./ C.1220	RCAF	20.08.42	27.06.43
S/L David L. RAMSAY	CAN./ C.937	RCAF	27.06.43	06.11.43
S/L George J. ELLIOTT	CAN./ C.1349	RCAF	07.11.43	...

SQUADRON USAGE

Formed initially as No. 11 (Army Co-operation) Squadron in October 1932 at Vancouver (British Columbia), this unit was renamed No. 111 (Coast Artillery Co-operation) Squadron on 15 November 1937. It was in this identity that it was mobilised on 10 September 1939. With the outbreak of war in Europe, 111 became even more active with the few Westland Lysanders then on charge. Concern for the security of the west coast was not the country's main concern, however. Even so, on 14 June 1940, No. 111 (CAC) Squadron was redesignated as No. 111 (F) Squadron but received no fighters, soldiering on with the Lysanders. It took on coastal-patrol duties and, while poorly equipped to go on the offensive, it did fly harbour patrols around Vancouver and Victoria. The European war had to be prepared for, though. On 1 February 1941, the squadron was disbanded. Most personnel were distributed among other local squadrons near Patricia Bay in British Columbia. On 3 November, the squadron re-formed at Rockliffe (Ottawa) as a fighter unit. The task of leading the new unit was given to S/L AD Nesbitt, a veteran of the Battle of Britain with No. 1 Squadron RCAF. The same day as re-formation, the first two Kittyhawks were delivered direct from the USA. Training began as pilots and groundcrew arrived at the squadron throughout the month. It was not an accident-free period, however, even though all incidents were reported as minor. Nevertheless, at the end of the month, 111 had already logged 90 hours and 15 minutes on the Kittyhawks. In early December, the squadron was split in to two flights: A Flight, to be led by F/O HT Mitchell (another Battle of Britain veteran); and B Flight, to be led by F/O AEL Cannon. With the attack on Pearl Harbor, however, the Pacific became a wider war zone and Canada was now on the front line. The RCAF therefore decided to re-task 111 (F) Squadron. It had begun training for duty in the European theatre but, suddenly, it was ordered west to the Pacific coast; training was discontinued on the 10th. Over the next two months, the squadron made its way across Canada, back to Patricia Bay on Vancouver Island. Its Kittyhawks were dismantled and shipped by rail. Reassembly took place at RCAF Sea Island and then the aircraft were flown over to Patricia Bay. The relocation of all the squadron's Kittyhawks and personnel was completed by late January. Considering the travel and erection of the Kittyhawks, the first flight from the new station was only undertaken on the 22nd; it was carried out by F/O Mitchell. More Kittyhawks were erected over the next few days and the number of flights increased. Sadly, on the 27th, Sgt CB Pierce was fatally injured when the aircraft he was flying, AK887, went into a spin and crashed and burned in front of a house in Vancouver. At the end of December 1941 and the beginning of January 1942, air activity was reduced owing to a shortage of glycol coolant. On 22 January, another accident occurred when the engine of AL180 caught fire, obliging its pilot, W/OL Orthman an American serving in the RCAF, to bale out at 3,000 feet. Fortunately, he landed safely while the Kittyhawk crashed into the sea and was lost. Later in the morning, another incident was recorded when Sgt Pidgeon hit a mound of dirt and stones at the end of the runway; as a result, the landing gear buckled and AK996 finished on its belly. Both pilot and aircraft lived to fly another day. Two days later, AK911 ground looped on landing, damaging the propeller. Despite this run of incidents, the squadron had 20 Kittyhawks on strength by the end of January and, with the glycol shortage alleviated by the middle of the month, intensive training could be resumed. In February, training continued while the final Kittyhawks were reassembled. Radio equipment was installed but a temporary shortage of earphones for the pilots' helmets initially limited usage. At the end of the month, 111 had developed something of a routine with its

Arthur Deane NESBITT
CAN./ C.1327

Deane Nesbitt, from Montreal, Quebec, joined the RCAF in September 1939 serving first with No. 115 Squadron, RCAF. Thanks to his experience with the Montreal Light Aeroplane Club, his training was swift and he was logically selected to be sent to the UK in June 1940 with No. 1 Squadron, RCAF. He participated in the Battle of Britain, claiming three aircraft destroyed between 26 August and 15 September, but was shot down on the 15th. He managed to bail out but was wounded and would spend the next three weeks in hospital.

In March 1941, Nesbitt took command of No. 401 (RCAF) Squadron, formerly No. 1 Squadron RCAF, and led it until mid-September. He made no further claims but during that period but, at the end of his command, he was awarded the DFC. He returned to Canada soon after. In Canada, he was given command of No. 111 Squadron RCAF, in November, while it was being re-formed on Curtiss Kittyhawks. He led the squadron until June 1942 to lead 'Y' Wing in the Aleutians until October. Promoted to Wing Commander, Nesbitt served in various non-operational positions during the next two years before sailing to the UK to become the WingCo Flying of No. 144 (RCAF) Wing, between May and July 1944, before being posted to No. 83 GSU. In January 1945, he was appointed OC of No. 143 (RCAF) Wing as a Group Captain and he would remain there until September 1945. Repatriated to Canada, he was released from service in November that year.

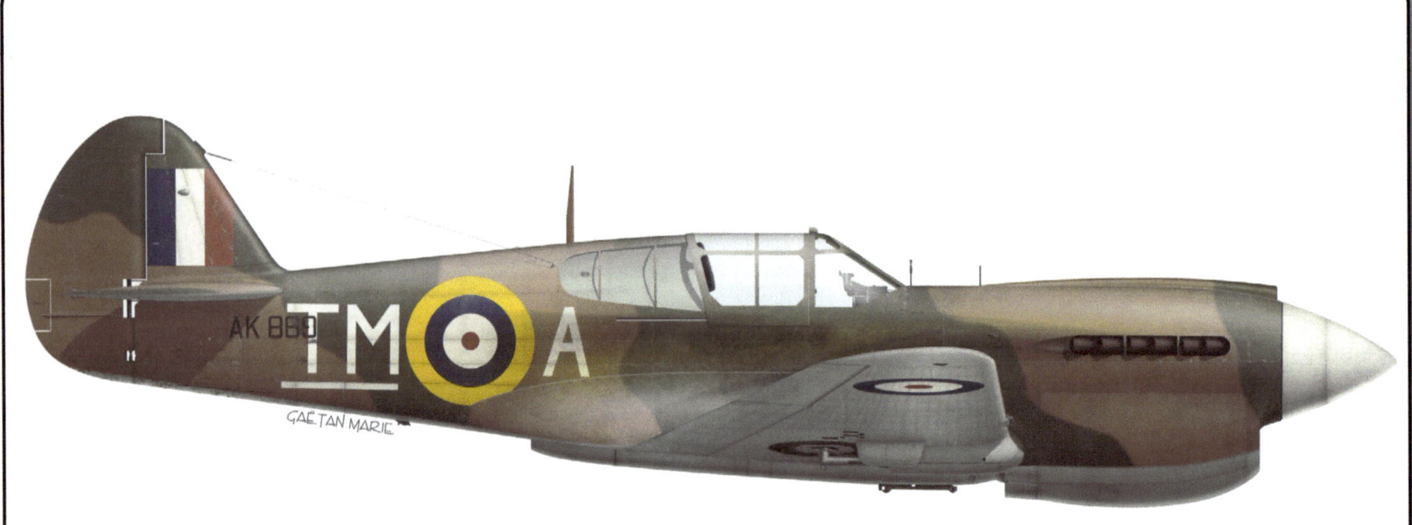

Curtiss Kittyhawk Mk I AK869
No. 111 Squadron, RCAF
Patricia Bay, British Columbia (Canada), spring 1942

Seen at Patricia Bay in the spring of 1942, Kittyhawk Mk.I AK869 wears the initial 'TM' squadron codes. *(Andrew Thomas)*

force of 20 Kittyhawks. Close to 450 hours were flown including some squadron formation flights, the first since the unit was formed. In the following weeks, the squadron lost some of its pilots as they were posted out to help form other RCAF squadrons; they were replaced by freshly graduated flyers. Sadly, Sgt D Stapleton was killed when he crashed in AL212 while practicing air-to-ground firing on 19 April. The squadron lost another Kittyhawk and pilot a month later when, during a practice scramble on 12 May, Sgt Richard RT Christy developed engine trouble at 3,000 feet. He tried to return to base but crashed into the sea near James Island. The aircraft sank like a stone and Christy drowned. Besides those incidents, 111 remained active between January and May 1942, gaining valuable operational experience flying coastal patrols and building experience in the P-40's capabilities. The threat was real as nine Japanese submarines had been patrolling the coastline from California to Alaska and the Aleutians. Tensions were high in the United States and Canada. In May, anticipating a Japanese attack on the US naval base at Dutch Harbor, on Unalaska Island in the Aleutians, the United States built a secret airfield on Umnak Island, just west of Unalaska. On 3 June, the Japanese raided Dutch Harbor. This could have been either a prelude to a major invasion of US territory or just a diversionary tactic. In any case, the Japanese initiative was considered significant. Soon after, the Japanese occupied two Aleutian islands, Attu and Kiska, where they installed a large garrison of troops. Called to reinforce the USAAF in Alaska, 111 was kept busy in June packing for transfer to Elmendorf Field, Anchorage. Twelve pilots and machines, accompanied by a Hudson carrying ground crews for the Kittyhawks, left for Sea Island on the 3rd. After several stops, the Kittyhawks arrived at Anchorage on the 8th; some of the aircraft were delayed by technical failures, however, but not for long. The next day, the squadron was based at Valdez but the squadron offices set up at Elmendorf. It would maintain its main base there until 30 October. On 12 June, No. 111 (F) Squadron linked up with No. 8 (Bomber Reconnaissance) Squadron to form X Wing while Y Wing formed with No. 118 (F) Squadron and No. 115 (BR) Squadron. Squadron Leader Nesbitt, now with a DFC to his name, was promoted to the job of wing commander of Y Wing. Gordon R McGregor became wing commander of X Wing. Upon Nesbitt's departure, F/L JW Kerwin, another Battle of Britain veteran, assumed command. The two bomber squadrons flew Bristol Bolingbroke Mk.IVs.

Early in July, 111 Squadron was told to detach 12 Kittyhawks, 21 pilots and 60 ground crew for a move to Umnak Island, the forward airbase. They would remain on Umnak until 12 October; their task would be to fly defensive patrols around Umnak and Unalaska. By taking over defensive duties, they would be relieving USAAF squadrons to carry the fight to the Japanese forces on Adak, Kiska and Attu Islands. For the remaining aircraft and personnel, 111 took over readiness on the 15th with six Kittyhawks. However, the rest of the month proved quiet, and the first alert occurred on 1 July; an uneventful scramble (later identified as a Bolingbroke) was followed by a second at lunch time, this one successful but the 'bogey' was, once again, a Bolingbroke. Meanwhile, the detachment's departure was planned for 13 July, with six Kittyhawks, led by W/C McGregor, leaving Elmendorf for Umnak and Cold Bay. On the way to Naknak, F/Sgt G Schwalm was forced to bale out due to failure of his electrical system and, on arrival at Naknak, P/O RL Lynch crashed on landing. Schwalm was picked up several hours later; McGregor returned to Elmendorf to collect two more pilots and aircraft on the 14th. The 15th saw no flying because of bad weather and the ferry continued the next day. McGregor led the Kittyhawks from Naknak for Cold Bay at 10:00 hours, accompanied by the two transports, arriving at 12:00 hours. At 13:30 hours, one of the transports, piloted by Capt Fillmore, left Cold Bay for Umnak and, soon after, the weather was reported as suitable. Half an hour after Fillmore's departure, the Kittyhawks took off for Umnak. Shortly after passing Dutch Harbor, the aircraft ran into bad weather; fog was ahead, behind and on the starboard side. McGregor gave the order to turn back but, owing to the low ceiling (50 feet), the others lost him in the turn and went into the fog. McGregor landed at Cold Bay and the Kittyhawk piloted by P/O OJ Eskil arrived at Umnak. The remaining five were lost. In the end, two transports and nine pilots, one medical officer and 17 men arrived at Umnak. McGregor attempted to locate the missing pilots from a Catalina, but to no avail, owing to the hopeless weather conditions. Finally, two crash sites were found on a hillside the next day and the bodies of P/O DE Whiteside (AL201/H) and F/Sgt FR Lennon, an American from New Jersey (AL138/G) brought back to Umnak. A wider search was launched and two more bodies were found, S/L Kerwin (AK954/E) and Sgt SR Maxmen (AK996/S), on Unalaska on the 22nd. The remaining missing pilot, F/Sgt GDR Baird (AL166/O), was never found and was declared lost at sea.

On 19 July, it was decided that, since the American forces on Umnak Island were up to strength in terms of aircraft but short of pilots, the ten remaining 111 pilots would fly USAAF P-40Es. These men became part of 'Flight F' of the 11th Pursuit Squadron. They retained their identity as RCAF officers and their borrowed aircraft were given RCAF and squadron markings. The squadron remained without an official CO for about a month until S/L KA Boomer arrived on 20 August. In the meantime, 111 was kept busy flying patrols almost every day using the USAAF P-40Es. Four days later, two new P-40Ks were tested and reported as an improvement over the P-40E. In the afternoon, F/O Lynch and F/Sgt EA Merkley were the first to use the P-40Ks on patrol, mush to their resulting great satisfaction. At the end of the month, the squadron had 16 P-40Es and seven P-40Ks on hand, back to full strength. Daily patrols from Umnak and Elmendorf were the routine as far as weather permitted. On the 25th the CO, Lynch, F/O JG Gohl and P/O HO Gooding took part in a raid on Kiska, the first offensive operation made by 111 in Alaska. They left Umnak on the 22nd as part of a force of nine B-24s, 12 P-39s and 20 P-40s to bomb and strafe Kiska. They refueled at Fierplace; the raid was to be completed the following day. However, an hour in, bad weather was encountered and the aircraft were forced to turn back; one American aircraft was lost in the process. Bad weather continued on the 24th and the second attempt finally got underway at 08.00 hours on 25 September. The weather was good throughout the trip. The formation arrived around 10.00 hours over Kiska harbour; the Canadian flight crossed Little Kiska Island, experiencing little ground fire from that point. Crossing the northern head of the harbour, they attacked naval gun emplacements and also several heavy strongpoints, continuing their attack to the main camp area. The CO and Gooding also attacked a Japanese radar station. Turning right, the formation crossed the northern head again and attacked gun emplacements. Inside the harbour area, a 'Zero' fighter floatplane (a 'Rufe') was encountered and immediately shot down by S/L Boomer. He climbed almost to a stall and pulled right up under the Japanese fighter. The floatplane caught fire and went down; Boomer saw the pilot jump just before the aircraft hit the sea. After circling the harbour, an enemy submarine was discovered and attacked by the Americans, who were soon joined by the Canadians. Thereafter, the Canadians and Americans headed home, landing at 11.50 hours, the former having expended all their ammunition. The claim made by Boomer would the only one made by the RCAF over North America and also the only air combat for a home-based RCAF squadron. Boomer was justifiably awarded an immediate DFC. This raid was the highlight of 111's stay at Elmendorf and Umnak as the squadron was relocated to Kodiak at the end of October to serve as part of the defensive force for the American base there. It would remain at Kodiak until 12 August 1943. From Kodiak, a detachment of six Kittyhawks was sent to Chiniak Point from 5 November 1942 until 24 April 1943, and another detachment of eight returned to Umnak from 2 May to 12 June 1943. At the end of 1942, and the beginning of 1943, 111 was operating a force of about 12 P-40s (more or less evenly balanced between E and K models) and 12 RCAF pilots, four of them having American connections. Activity otherwise reduced and besides the wreck of 42-45954 on 20 February, when F/O Delbert F English slid on ice on the runway and crashed into a steel emplacement, there was not much to report even though some strafing sorties were carried out.

A major change in X Wing took place on 3 March 1943 when 14 Squadron, also flying P-40Ks, replaced 8 Squadron. The decision was made because the Bolingbroke bombers (Canadian-built Blenheims) were subject to an impossibly long supply line and suffered from a lack of replacement and maintenance parts. Consequently, they were not as useful as the rugged P-40 for which there was a ready supply of replacement parts because the same type was being used by the USAAF in Alaska and the Aleutians. In May, a group of ten pilots and eight P-40K-1s from 111 Squadron were deployed to Amchitka Island where they were part of the continuing offensive against the Japanese on Kiska. This deployment ended on 12 July, the squadron returning to rejoin the group on Kodiak. In the meantime, at the end of June, S/L Boomer was posted to Western Air Command; he was replaced by F/L DL Ramsay. In July, eight P-40s were transferred to 14 Squadron at Umnak and five others were sent to X Wing at Anchorage while some of the unit's personnel were transferred to 14 Squadron in July and August. What remained of 111 was repatriated to Canada and sent to Patricia Bay on 14 August. By that time, the Japanese had abandoned Kiska, quietly slipping away in the fog.

Reformation was slow, as was re-equipment: only two P-40Ns, 2105867 and 2105869, were taken on charge on 17 September. More arrived, including three P-40Es (1047, 1051 and 1066). The turnover of aircraft continued as orders were received to transfer six P-40Ns to No. 163 Squadron; three P-40Es from 14 Squadron and six from No. 118 Squadron were planned to be received in exchange. On 18 October, Kittyhawks 861, 862 and 863 were handed over while 729, 1057, 1095 and 1098 were added and, on 25 October, 866 and 867 left. At the end of October, the squadron had 11 P-40Es and three P-40Ns on hand. During that period of time, the unit performed mainly army support duties. A new CO, S/L GJ Elliott, also took over, but the Battle of Britain veteran's command was brief as 111 was selected as one of the six home-based fighter units for overseas duty. On 12 November, the squadron flew its last operational sorties: two Kittyhawks scrambled from Patricia Bay to intercept an unidentified aircraft that proved to be friendly. In total, despite terribly harsh flying conditions, the squadron had flown 598 operational sorties in its brief existence. This was an impressive effort given most days in the Aleutians saw weather that no one could fly in. Sent to the UK, it was redesignated No. 440 (RCAF) Squadron and equipped with Typhoons (see *SQUADRONS! 56*).

Claims - 111 Squadron, RCAF (Confirmed and Probable)

Date	Pilot	SN	Origin	Type	Serial	Code	Nb	Cat.
25.09.42	S/L Kenneth A. **Boomer**	Can./ C.1220	RCAF	A6M2-N			1.0	C

Total: 1.0

Kenneth Arthur Boomer
Can./ C.1220

A Canadian from Ontario, Ken Boomer enlisted in the RCAF in October 1939 as a regular air force officer. He was trained in Canada before he was posted at the end of the summer of 1940 to No. 112 Squadron RCAF, then an Army co-operation unit, based in the UK. He then joined No. 1 Squadron RCAF to fly Hurricanes. This unit was re-designated No. 401 (RCAF) Squadron on 1 March 1941. In June he left for No. 411 (RCAF) Squadron on its formation to serve as a flight commander. He made his first claim, a probable Ju88 on 7 November, this claim being upgraded to confirmed victory later on. In March 1942, tour expired, he was sent home and joined No. 132 Squadron RCAF as OC at the end of April. In August he joined No. 111 Squadron RCAF as OC in Alaska flying Kittyhawks and here he was to make the only confirmed claim (on 25 September) over a Japanese aircraft by a Canadian pilot during the Aleutians campaign. A DFC was awarded in January 1943. In June 1943 he left his command and took various non-operational postings. In April 1944 he returned to the UK and attended No. 60 OTU to gain experience on Mosquito intruder operations. He was posted to No. 418 (RCAF) Squadron in August to fly the Mosquito Mk.VI. On 22 October he was sent out on a Day Ranger operation, with navigator Flight Lieutenant N.J. Gibbons, in Mosquito PZ198. They presumably destroyed one enemy aircraft and damaged another, both on the ground, before contact was lost and they did not return.

Curtiss Kittyhawk Mk I AL194
No. 111 Squadron, RCAF
Umnak Island, Alaska (USA), spring 1943

111 Squadron pilots posing in front of a P-40 K-1-CU, July 7,1943. The squadron departed Amchitka two days later.
They are: L-R: F/O H.L. Gooding (later OC 440 Sqn), W/O1 E.A. Merkley (†19.11.43, 57 OTU), F/L J.G. Gohl (†12.06.44, 440 Sqn), P/O W.L. Pigden, P/O J.H. Clarke (14 Squadron), W/O F.R.F. Skelly (†22.01.45, 438 Sqn), S/L D.L Ramsay (OC), P/O H.F. Morse (14 Squadron), W/C R.E.E Morrow (X Wing), W/O N. Stusiak (†27.05.44, 440 Sqn), F/O G.G. Millar (†28.09.44, 442 Sqn), F/O S.V Garside (†07.06.44, 440 Sqn), P/O W.R. Campbell (†01.08.44, 442 Sqn), P/O W.R. Weeks, W/O C.O.R. Clacken, Sgt W.D. Peacock, W/O2 F.J. Crowley (†11.11.44, 440 Sqn), W/O2 S.R.J. McLeod.

Fort Greely, Kodiak, Alaska;
Probably mid-July, 1943

111 Squadron Pilots: W/O F.R.F. Skelly (†22.01.45, 438 Sqn), W/O2 F.J. Crowley (†11.11.44, 440 Sqn), W/O2 S.R.J. McLeod, W/O1 E.A. Merkley (†19.11.43, 57 OTU), F/L H.O Gooding (later OC 440 Sqn), P/O C.W. Hicks (†08.08.44, 440 Sqn), F/L J.G. Gohl (†12.06.44, 440 Sqn), W/O N. Stusiak (†27.05.44, 440 Sqn).

Date	Pilot	S/N	Origin	Serial	Code	Fate
27.12.41	Sgt Charles B. **PIERCE**	CAN./ R.84163	RCAF	**AK887**		†
19.04.42	Sgt Douglas L. **STAPLETON**	CAN./ R.103254	RCAF	**AL212**		†
12.05.42	Sgt Richard R.T. **CHRISTYE**	CAN./ R.106837	RCAF	**AK881**		†
23.06.42	W/O2 Luke T. **ORTHMAN**	CAN./ R.54047	(US)/RCAF	**AK869**		-
16.07.42	S/L John W. **KERWIN**	CAN./ C.922	RCAF	**AK954**	LZ-F	†
	Sgt Stanley R. **MAXMEN**	CAN./ R.100245	RCAF	**AK996**	LZ-S	†
	F/Sgt Frank R. **LENNON**	CAN./ R.79072	(US)/RCAF	**AL138**	LZ-G	†
	F/Sgt Gordon D.R. **BAIRD**	CAN./ R.95331	RCAF	**AL166**	LZ-O	†
	P/O Dean E. **WHITESIDE**	CAN./ J.10607	RCAF	**AL201**	LZ-H	†
17.07.42	F/Sgt George T. **SCHWALM**	CAN./ R.85578	RCAF	**AK989**		-
01.12.43	F/O Stanley V. **GARSIDE**	CAN./ J.5068	RCAF	**1080**		-

Total: 11

Upon its arrival in Alaska, No. 111 Squadron was given new 'LZ' codes. Here, three P-40Es patrol over the mountainous landscape of Alaska. The Kittyhawk leading is AL109/LZ-V, followed by AK905/LZ-D and AK940/LZ-E.

Some of No. 111 Squadron's Kittyhawks soon after their arrival in Alaska. AK996/LZ-S and AK954/LZ-F are visible.
In October 1942, squadron codes were discontinued; only the individual letters were kept. In the foreground is Kittyhawk 1047/T. To its side is 1035/C. They are seen in June 1943 shortly after the RCAF had allotted new serials.

Kittyhawk 1047/T having its engine warmed before a flight over the Aleutians. Weather conditions were tough on personnel and equipment.

Adopted on 17 March 1942, the Thunderbird totem of the west coast tribes appeared on some of No. 111 Squadron's P-40s, like AL194/V which suffered an accident on 13 April 1943 at Miller Army Airfield, Chiniak Point, Kodiak Island, Alaska. The American pilot, W/O Samuel RJ MacLeod, was uninjured.

By the end of its time in Alaska, No. 111 Squadron had shark's mouths painted on some of its Kittykawks, as seen here on 1071/A but that was later discontinued as we can see on 729/E in November 1943.

OTHER UNITS

NO. 118 SQUADRON (SQUADRON CODES: RE, VW)

After having been equipped with Gloster Goblins (see *SQUADRONS! 09*), a type that was totally obsolete as a fighter, 118 Squadron began its conversion to the P-40 in November 1941. By that time, it was based at Dartmouth in Nova Scotia and the CO was S/L Hartland de Molson, assisted by two fellow Battle of Britain veterans, Flight Lieutenants BD Russel and AM Yuile. The CO and the A Flight commander, Russel, were among the pilots who tested the first Kittyhawks on 8 November; with the arrival of more P-40s, training soon got underway. By the end of the month, 12 Kittyhawks were on hand but not yet operational. The first incident occurred on 2 December when Kittyhawk AK827 crashed on the aerodrome. The pilot, P/O EB Hart escaped injury and the P-40 was later repaired. At the end of February 1942, 118 had a remarkable seven Goblins, 15 Kittyhawks (AK773, AK779, AK785, AK791, AK797, AK803, AK809, AK815, AK821, AK833, AK839, AK845, AK857, AL216 and AL222) and eight Hurricanes in its inventory. During that month, the Kittyhawk saw its operational debut with a scramble on the 16th by F/O Dean (AK785) and P/O Handley (AK815); like the scrambles that followed, it was uneventful. The unit settled into a routine until June when it was transferred from Eastern Command to Western Command and Patricia Bay in British Columbia, wrecking one Kittyhawk during a practice flight before the move was made, AK791 causing the death of Sgt GH Isralson on 10 March. This move was just a step on the way to Annette Island in Alaska. There, the squadron was placed under Y Wing. The ferry was achieved under the supervision of the now S/L Yuile, the new CO. More operational sorties were flown on the west coast even though they were limited to defensive work. On 12 October, Kittyhawk AL210, flown by P/O GAG Baxter, was reported missing. While in a practice formation, Baxter's seat dinghy accidently inflated. He was unable to overcome the pressure created and died when his aircraft crashed a mile east of Dall Head. Ten days later, AK797 crashed when its right wheel collapsed, causing a ground loop and resulting in the aircraft leaving the runway and piling up on some rocks in a ditch. It was a lucky escape for Sgt LD Manser as, after an investigation, the Kittyhawk was not repaired and struck off charge in June 1943. It was a busy day for the squadron as, that evening, F/O Arthur Jarred saw what he thought was the periscope of a submarine and fired a few bursts at what was found to be a floating log. No further major incidents were reported until 26 January 1943 when P/O AB Newsome had a narrow escape from serious injury when the engine of his aircraft (AL227) burst into flames on approach for landing. The flames spread through the cockpit before Newsome could extricate himself, resulting in burns to his face and destroying most of his clothing. A couple of days later, it was the turn of F/O JR Beirnes to wreck another Kittyhawk, when he collided on landing run with the aircraft flown F/O WN Stowe on return from a local flying. At the end of February, a change of command took place with F/L FG Grant taking over. A month later, a memorial service was held for four men killed in a Norseman crash two days before; among them was No. 115 Squadron's OC (S/L Fred B Curry). In the afternoon, after the ceremony, the bodies were loaded on board a Dakota to be flown south to Vancouver. Flight Lieutenant A Jarred, an American from Minnesota serving in the RCAF, and F/O JR Beirnes were authorised to escort the transport to the limits of the local flying area but, shortly after he was airborne, F/L Jarred spun in after stalling at the top of an upward roll. He was killed when the aircraft crashed a mile north-west of the runway at Annette Island. The crash was attributed to an attempted roll with a 300-lb bomb attached to the belly of the aircraft (AK821). The squadron remained at Annette until mid-August when a transfer to Sea Island was ordered. Dawn and dusk patrols resumed on 17 August but only for a short time as the squadron had been selected to reinforce the RCAF overseas. The final patrols were carried out on 29 September, after which the unit began preparations for the move to the UK where it became No. 438 (RCAF) Squadron flying Typhoons (see *SQUADRONS! 56*).

Summary of the aircraft lost by accident - 118 Squadron, RCAF

Date	Pilot	S/N	Origin	Serial	Code	Fate
10.03.42	Sgt Glenn H. **ISRALSON**	CAN./ R.61989	RCAF	**AK791**		†
12.10.42	P/O George G.A. **BAXTER**	CAN./ J.10635	RCAF	**AL210**		†
23.10.42	F/Sgt Leo D. **MANZER**	CAN./ R.99658	RCAF	**AK797**		-
14.02.43	F/O Jack R. **BEIRNES**	CAN./ C.13458	RCAF	**AL226**		-
28.03.43	F/L Arthur **JARRED**	CAN./ C.4808	(US)/RCAF	**AK821**		†

Total: 5

Arthur McLeod YUILE
CAN./ C.1328

Joining the RCAF in September 1939, Yuile's training was advanced enough by June 1940 for him to embark with No. 1 Squadron RCAF to the UK. There, he completed his operational training and, in August, flew his first operational sorties. On 1 September, he was shot down unhurt but had his revenge on the 11th by shooting down an He111. On the 27th, he claimed a Do17 as damaged. He remained with the squadron until mid-February 1941 and was then repatriated, joining No. 118 Squadron RCAF at Ottawa soon after as a flight commander. In April 1942, he was given command of No. 126 Squadron RCAF, but was recalled to command 118 Squadron in June 1942, as it was about to leave for Alaska, due to his experience in the Battle of Britain. He eventually left the unit in February 1943. No further operational command positions followed. Yuile eventually left the service in September 1944 to complete his studies at McGill University.

Curtiss Kittyhawk Mk I AL224
No. 118 Squadron, RCAF
Annette Island, Alaska (USA), summer 1942

This page and the next one: Various scenes showing No. 118 Squadron about to depart for the west coast and Alaska in June 1942. Among the Kittyhawks that can be identified is AK803/RE-K, later reserialled 1034. Other Kittyhawks visible are AK773/RE-C, AK845/RE-X

This page and the next one: Once in Alaska, the codes were changed from 'RE' to 'VW'. Kittyhawk AK857/VW-H was damaged on 1 September but was repaired, became 1043 in the RCAF system and later served later with No. 133 Squadron. It was struck off charge in August 1946. Kittyhawk AL224/VW-N also served with 133 Squadron but, as 1096, was involved in an accident on 25 June 1944.

This unit was formed at Mont-Joli, Quebec, on 1 May 1942 but personnel began to arrive about a month before. The squadron was equipped from the start with both Kittyhawks and Hurricanes. The new CO, S/L Joseph AJ Chevrier, a Battle of Britain veteran with No. 1 Squadron RCAF, arrived on 1 May. As personnel continued to join, the squadron still had no fighters on hand, so began to train on Harvards. Six Kittyhawks were in storage on the base, but the CO didn't have the authorisation to use them as those aircraft had not been officially accepted by the RCAF. Authorisation came on the 8th and Kittyhawks AK865, AK914, AK915, AK930, AK933 and AL136 were taken on charge. The first to be test flown was AK915 on the 12th. The others followed in the next few days. The squadron was working up to operational status but, on 6 July, a call from the Royal Canadian Navy was received requesting assistance in locating a submarine that had sunk two vessels off Cap-Chat. Four Kittyhawks were made ready and armed. The four pilots that participated were the CO, F/L AEL Cannon, Sgt WL Pigden and Sgt JG Bertrand. Sadly, only three Kittyhawks returned, all almost out of fuel; S/L Chevrier was posted missing. It was later discovered he had run out of petrol and was killed when he ditched AK915 1.5 miles off Sainte-Anne in the Saint Lawrence River. He was replaced the next day by F/L Cannon. A week later, 130 moved to Saguenay (Bagotville), where it would remain for over a year; no replacement aircraft arrived to make up for the Kittyhawk lost. The squadron continued to use the five remaining Kittyhawks as its main equipment (complemented by Harvards) until September when it began its transition to the Hurricane. This was achieved in early October, the Kittyhawks leaving on the 8th (see *SQUADRONS 26!*)

Summary of the aircraft lost by accident - 130 Squadron, RCAF

Date	Pilot	S/N	Origin	Serial	Code	Fate
06.07.42	S/L J.A.J. **Chevrier**	Can./ C.856	RCAF	**AK915**		†
		Total: 1				

Jacques Chevrier enlisted in the RCAF in July 1938. He was sent to the UK as a replacement pilot and joined No. 1 Squadron at the end of October. He returned to Canada in January 1941 where he became ADC to His Excellency the Governor-General, the Earl of Athlone, between August 1941 and March 1942. He was then given command of 130 Sqn on its formation. On 6 July 1942, Chevrier led four Kittyhawks to search for U-boats after a freighter was torpedoed 10 miles off Sainte-Anne-des-Monts (Quebec). Chevrier ran out of fuel on return to Mont-Joli and died when his Kittyhawk (AK915) ditched in the St. Lawrence just off Sainte-Anne-des-Monts. His body was never recovered.

<u>**No. 132 Squadron**</u>

This unit was formed at Rockliffe (Ottawa) on 14 April 1942 and, from the beginning, was planned to be equipped with Kittyhawks. The first commander was F/L AEL Cannon, who arrived on the 21st, but was soon replaced by S/L KA Boomer on the 27th. The month was spent accepting the aircraft and, at the end of April, the squadron had three Kittyhawk Mk.Is and seven Harvards on hand. This had increased to 14 Kittyhawks a month later and the number of hours flown exceeded 800 (including hours flown on Harvards). Intended to defend the west coast of Canada, a move to Sea Island in British Columbia was made on 4 June, followed by another to Patricia Bay on 17 July. Training had continued in the meantime, with an accident on 26 May (aircraft wrecked, but pilot uninjured), but the first fatal accident was recorded on 12 July when Sgt CL O'Hara was killed when ET863 crashed about a quarter mile east of Woodward's Hill. The cause was never determined with certainty. A month later, during another training flight, the engine of ET852 caught fire and the pilot, Sgt APC Diadato, was forced to bale out; he was injured and knocked out when he struck the fin. He fortunately recovered consciousness and made a perfect landing in the water, from where he was picked up, thanks to his squadronmate, P/O DC Stults, who raised the alarm. The search proved difficult as Stults soon lost sight of Diadato in the haze. In the meantime, 132 had a new commanding officer, S/L George J Elliott, who took over when S/L Boomer was posted to No. 111 Squadron in Alaska. A move to Tofino was organised on 16 October but just before that a tragedy occurred when, while on a scramble, F/L John D Butler in ET860 and F/O GP Johnson in AL216 collided. They were accompanied by P/O LV Kirsh in ET849. The weather was bad and visibility reduced but fog was soon discovered ahead of the formation. Butler ordered a reversal of course but it was not completed before the formation entered the fog. The collision occurred soon after; only Kirsh managed to escape. The squadron suffered another mid-air collision and the loss of two more pilots in November. On the 28th, a section of three Kittyhawks led by F/L MW Hees took off with a Harvard, the trainer having a cameraman of the official press party on board. They were flying at 50 feet when the aircraft flown by Hees (ET849) struck the tail of the Harvard with its right wing. The Harvard went into a shallow dive and burst into flames; P/O RW Rogers and L Roy, the cameraman, were both killed in the Harvard, while the Kittyhawk was seen climbing before rolling into a sort of barrel roll with pieces falling away; it then dived into a cleared area, exploding on impact. Hoes did not survive. The beginning of 1943 was quiet. On 7 March, the squadron received a 13th Kittyhawk, the highest number on hand since formation the previous April; 132 had been operational with only eight Kittyhawks between September and January 1943. The new aircraft was a P-40M (Kittyhawk III). Two weeks later, three more Kittyhawk IIIs were accepted, bringing the number to 16, the normal establishment of a fighter squadron. On 15 May, the squadron received notification that, from that date, it would be used to train pilots for posting to operational squadrons in Alaska, a kind of post-OTU. On 1 July, the squadron was given a new home, Boundary Bay and soon after, Kittyhawk 1049 was lost in an accident, the pilot, P/O MA Foster being killed. Until November, the year passed smoothly and, other than some minor accidents, no major events were reported. However, on 5 November, 132 was taking part in dogfight training involving four Kittyhawks and four USN Hellcats. Pilot Officer KB Callaghan in Kittyhawk 833 collided with a Hellcat, causing both planes to crash; fortunately, both pilots baled out. The next day, S/L Elliott relinquished command to S/L JA Thompson who would lead 132 until its disbandment. The following month, Kittyhawk 842 was written off after it crashed on take-off; its pilot, P/O G Baker, was seriously injured with a fractured skull, back and elbow. In the following weeks, 132 recorded a succession of accidents. On 27 January, Kittyhawk 1081 was written-off after it was hit on the ground by Kittyhawk 723, which was taxiing too fast. The pilot of 723, P/O RW Rodmepl, escaped uninjured. On 24 February, Sgt FH Bell wrote off Kittyhawk 721 when its engine caught fire upon landing from a practice flight. Bell was slightly burned. The next month, the squadron returned to Tofino. It was not until 5 June that another major crash occurred, writing off 843. The pilot, P/O JP Dobereiner, was uninjured after an engine failure necessitated a forced landing. At the end of the month, the squadron was ordered to transfer five M-models (Kittyhawk III) to No. 5 OTU at Boundary Bay, starting on 1 July. In August, the squadron moved twice, to Patricia Bay then to Sea Island, the latter station being its last before disbandment on 30 September 1944. The final dusk patrol sorties were carried out a few days before, on the 21st, by F/O RL Abbott in 1084 and P/O HC Holm in 849. The patrol lasted an hour. In all, No. 132 Squadron flew over 1,400 operational sorties in two-and-a-half years.

Summary of the aircraft lost on Operations - 132 Squadron, RCAF

Date	Pilot	S/N	Origin	Serial	Code	Fate
06.10.42	F/L John D. **BUTLER**	CAN./ J.4245	RCAF	**ET860**		†
	F/O Gerald P. **JOHNSON**	CAN./ J.10430	RCAF	**AL216**		†

Total: 2

Date	Pilot	S/N	Origin	Serial	Code	Fate
26.05.42	Sgt Albert A. **Watkins**	Can./ R.107984	RCAF	**ET854**		-
12.07.42	Sgt Charles L. **O'Hara**	Can./ R.119372	RCAF	**ET863**		†
16.08.42	Sgt Albert PC. **Diodato**	Can./ R.111035	RCAF	**ET852**		-
28.11.42	F/L Macleod W. **Hees**	Can./ C.1468	RCAF	**ET849**		†
27.07.43	P/O Milton A. **Foster**	Can./ J.23363	RCAF	**1059**		†
05.11.43	F/O Keith B. **Callaghan**	Can./ J.26403	RCAF	**833**		†
18.12.42	F/O Gordon **Baker**	Can./ J.35976	RCAF	**842**		**Inj.**
27.01.44	*Ground collision while parked*	-	RCAF	**1081**		-
24.02.44	Sgt Frank H. **Bell**	Can./ R.167459	RCAF	**721**		-
05.06.44	F/O John P. **Dobereiner**	Can./ J.39549	RCAF	**843**		-

Total: 10

Taken on charge in January 1943, Kittyhawk 831 was issued to No. 132 Squadron and coded 'C'. It flew with the unit until its disbandment, then served with No. 8 OTU for a short time before moving to the Fighter Affiliation Flight of No. 5 OTU.

Formed in June 1942 at Lethbridge in Alberta, the unit moved to British Columbia in October 1942 where it became operational on Hurricanes. On 11 March 1944, the squadron moved from Tofino to Sea Island, using the Hurricanes to ferry the pilots as conversion to former No. 163 Squadron Kittyhawks was about to take place. The squadron was under the command of S/L WC Connell, a Battle of Britain veteran. Conversion was undertaken quickly and, by the end of March, the squadron had 11 Kittyhawk Mk.Is, two Mk.IAs and five Mk.IIIs on hand. On 24 April, S/L Connell was posted out and temporary command was given to F/L RW Ferguson pending the arrival of S/L IC Ormston who assumed command on 12 June. On 21 May 1944, a first fatal accident was recorded, when P/O DK Sundercok was killed while practicing aerobatics. One month later, while taxiing for a dawn patrol, a ground collision occurred between P/O RJ Johnston in 1096 and F/O FP Clegg in 836. Both aircraft caught fire and Clegg was killed instantly; Johnston escaped injury. In July, the Kittyhawk IIIs were replaced by brand-new Kittyhawk IVs. On 18 August, while on a scramble, P/O JT Wilkie, in Kittyhawk 731, went into a violent spin at 6,000 feet. He started to get out and struck his leg on the canopy hood, severely injuring it below the knee. His parachute opened normally, however, and he was picked up by a fishing smack after landing in the water. A few days later, 133 lost another Kittyhawk, this time during a formation practice. The engine of Kittyhawk 863 failed so the pilot, P/O RC Hughes, abandoned it and was rescued by a Canso soon after. In September, more incidents were recorded but the worst came on the 29th when Sgt G Paterson, an American from New York State, was posted missing from a dawn patrol. The wreckage of the Kittyhawk (1039) was found the same day but no trace of the pilot could be found. The following month, Kittyhawk 1031 had to be struck off charge after P/O A Shapiro landed violently and the aircraft bounced, resulting in a ground loop. Shapiro was uninjured, but the aircraft was not repaired. This bad run continued the next day with the write-off of Kittyhawk 1040 after the aircraft made a fast, flapless landing, went off the end of the runway and ditched. The pilot, Sgt AE Wice, survived. An electrical failure was responsible for the flaps not operating. This crash was followed by another when Sgt JG McLean in Kittyhawk 1053 ran out of fuel and had to make a forced landing three miles west of East Sound in the USA; despite the damage it sustained, the aircraft was not written off. The rest of the year fortunately passed without major incident.

January 1945 was quiet and all operations were carried out without the CO, who had been sent on a temporary posting elsewhere. Flight Lieutenant Ferguson commanded the unit in his absence, a time during which P/O DH Grundy was killed on the 14th during a practice flight. Ormston never actually returned and was eventually replaced by S/L JE Sheppard from the 31st. The routine was broken on 21 February when P/O EE Maxwell, flying 866/R, and F/O PV Brodeur, in 1041/C, scrambled after a Japanese fire balloon was located. They climbed to 25,000 feet and Maxwell shot it down near Patricia Bay; the wreckage landed on Sumas Mountain in Washington State. Another balloon was chased on 4 March but not intercepted. Pilot Officer JG Patten and Sgt Wise were luckier six days later when the former shot down a balloon at 13,500 feet near Patricia Bay. The squadron had begun to take the Mosquito on charge but only two had arrived by the end of the month. Activity was reduced over the next few months as the unit prepared for its conversion; pilots were sent to No. 7 OTU for that purpose. From the 19th, the few operational flights carried out were made by Mosquitoes. In mid-June, the number of Kittyhawks was reduced to six, but no hours were flown on the type during the month. Those last Kittyhawks eventually left the squadron in the first week of July.

Kittyhawk 729/C of No. 133 Squadron, the letter 'C' was assigned to it by No. 132 Squadron in 1942. Note the red maple leaf in the white circle. This insignia was more common with RCAF Overseas in Europe than in Canada itself. The individual letter was later changed to 'S'.

Ian Campbell ORMSTON
CAN./ J.5028

A Canadian from Montreal, Quebec, Ian Ormston enlisted in the RCAF in August 1940. Trained in Canada, he sailed to the UK in May 1941 where he attended OTU after which he was posted to No. 401 (RCAF) Squadron, in August 1941, as the unit was about to convert to the Spitfire. He served with this squadron until the end of his tour in July 1942, by which time he had become a flight commander and had claimed his first victories. Indeed, he opened his score in November 1941 by shooting down a Bf109 and added more, during the 'Channel Dash', on 12 February 1942. In May 1942, he was awarded the DFC and returned to Canada. After some months passed at No. 1 OTU as a flying instructor, he sailed once more to the UK in May 1943, to commence another tour, and rejoined 401 in June as a flight commander. He made his last claim on 19 July, a shared Fw190 probably destroyed, to bring his total to three confirmed victories (one shared), two probably destroyed (one shared) and one aircraft damaged. In September, he was posted to No. 411 (RCAF) Squadron as OC. At 22 years old, he was one of the youngest Canadian commanding officers. He led the squadron until 21 December 1943 when he was the victim of an accident on take off and was hospitalised with bad injuries to the spine. He was therefore repatriated and, upon recovery, was given command of No. 133 Squadron RCAF, based in British Columbia flying Kittyhawks, in June 1944. He relinquished command on 1 January 1945 and eventually left the service in April.

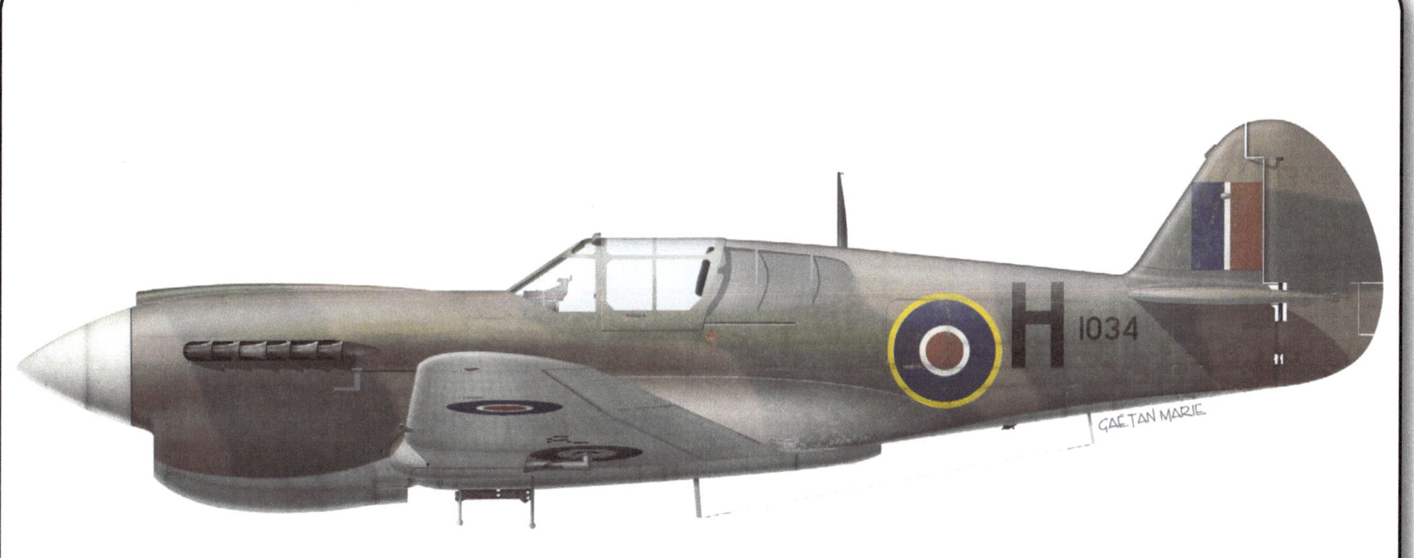

Curtiss Kittyhawk Mk I, 1034
No. 133 Squadron, RCAF
Tofino, British Columbia (Canada), autumn 1943

Date	Pilot	S/N	Origin	Serial	Code	Fate
25.06.44	P/O Frank P. **Clegg**	Can./ J.27302	RCAF	**836**		†
	P/O Robert J. **Johnston**	Can./ J.39550	RCAF	**1096**		-
18.08.44	P/O James T. **Wilkie**	Can./ J.39523	RCAF	**731**		**Inj.**
29.09.44	Sgt Gordon **Paterson**	Can./ R.190893	(us)/RCAF	**1039**		†

Total: 4

Date	Pilot	S/N	Origin	Serial	Code	Fate
21.05.44	P/O Donald K. **Sundercock**	Can./ J.38034	RCAF	**1087**		†
23.08.44	P/O Roderick C. **Hughes**	Can./ J.42271	RCAF	**863**		-
27.10.44	P/O Alec **Shapiro**	Can./ J.43302	RCAF	**1031**		-
28.10.44	Sgt AE. **Wice**	Can./ R.212570	RCAF	**1040**		-
14.01.45	P/O David H. **Grundy**	Can./ J.39524	RCAF	**726**		†

Total: 5

No. 133 Squadron's Kittyhawk 1034/H in flight. A Mk.I, it previously served with No. 118 Squadron.

Another Kittyhawk Mk.I of No 133 Squadron, formerly of No 118 Squadron, 1035/L is seen parked close to the control tower at Sea Island.

<u>**NO. 135 SQUADRON**</u>

Formed in June 1942 to defend the west coast of Canada, No. 135 Squadron was initially equipped with locally made Hurricanes, flying them until May 1944 when Curtiss Kittyhawks replaced them. The squadron was based at Patricia Bay in British Columbia at the time and the CO was S/L David J Smith.

The first two Kittyhawks, 848 and 855, were tested on 8 May. Acceptance checks continued over the next few days while conversion flights were undertaken. By the end of the month, 135 had 17 Kittyhawk IVs (846, 847/B, 848/P, 849, 854, 855, 856, 858/J, 859/K, 860/H, 861, 862/C, 865/U, 871, 872/S, 873, 874, 875/A and 879/X) and 13 Hurricanes on hand but the latter were awaiting their departure for further allocation. During this interim period, little operational flying was carried out, but the Kittyhawks were ready to take over the work of the Hurricanes. On 19 May, a morning scramble was ordered and F/L AE Harvey in 848 and P/O JR McBain in 854 took off, marking the operational debut of the Kittyhawk with the squadron in the process. In the afternoon, there were two six-aircraft scrambles, but nothing was reported. Routine was paramount during Summer 1944 and, apart from some minor accidents, things remained quiet until the end of the year. Over 2,500 hours were flown on the Kittyhawks in 1944. The year 1945 started as the second half of 1944 had finished – routine flying. However, on 22 February, while on dusk patrol, F/O CE Harvill experienced electrical failure and was forced to land at Ault Field, Whidbey Island, in the USA. At the time, the field's length was limited and while Harvill got his wheels down, he could not lower his flaps; consequently, he ran off the end of the runway into a pool of mud at the end of a ten-foot embankment. Harvill was uninjured and the aircraft severely damaged; no repairs were undertaken. On 11 April, F/L Andrew R MacKenzie, one of the two flight commanders, became the CO. Five days later, disaster was just avoided on return from a practice bombing sortie. While the six Kittyhawks were landing in sections, F/O S Stratapettie in 872 swerved to the wrong side of the runway and collided with Kittyhawk 855 piloted by F/O JWL Philipps. Flying Officer KG Graham, in Kittyhawk 854, landing behind those two, was forced to apply his brakes harshly to avoid a further collision and ended up on his nose. All the aircraft were repaired. Also, on 20 April, the last interception of a balloon took place when P/O PV Brodeur, out of Abbotsford, shot one down over Vedder Mountain. A month later, during an aircraft test, F/O S Dixon, while making a curving fighter approach to land, undershot the runway and the left wingtip of 846 struck the ground. The pilot escaped uninjured, but the aircraft was only good for scrap. The outcome of the accident on the 24th was, unfortunately, worse. Kittyhawk 861, flown by F/O T Cormie, was seen to crash, from a height of 10,000 feet, two miles south of the aerodrome at Patricia Bay, presumably after its pilot lost control. On 5 June, S/L Jackson E Sheppard assumed command to become 135's final CO. Two more accident was experienced until the squadron disbanded on 10 September 1945 (F/O WD Ford on scramble and F/L PL Gibbs during a training flight, both safe), the last hours being logged on 23 August. Over 4,000 hours were flown on Kittyhawks in 1945. At the time of disbandment, the squadron was using the following Kittyhawks: 727 (a Mk.IA), 847/B, 850/D, 853, 854, 856, 857/V, 859/K, 862/C, 864/F, 865/U, 866/R, 868, 872/S, 873 and 880/N.

Jack Sheppard enlisted in the RCAF in August 1939 as ground-crew. Accepted for pilot training a year later, he was trained in Canada and sailed to the UK in August 1941 with a commission. He attended No. 53 OTU and then joined No. 43 Squadron for his first operational assignment. His stay was brief as he volunteered to serve with the Merchant Ship Fighter Unit in December. In February 1943, Sheppard was posted to No. 401 (RCAF) Squadron where he made his first claim on 26 November, an Fw190 destroyed; he had been granted a flight commander's position with the unit in July. Other claims followed in the first months of 1944. In April, he was given command of No. 412 (RCAF) Squadron and, in the next few months, added two aircraft destroyed, on 10 May and 2 July, to bring his score to five confirmed victories. Shot down on 2 August, he evaded capture and was back a few days later but did not return to operations and was repatriated to Canada instead with a DFC. After a period of rest, he was posted to No. 133 Squadron as CO in January 1945, leaving in May to take over No. 135 Squadron. He commanded the unit until its disbandment in September. Sheppard left the service in February 1946.

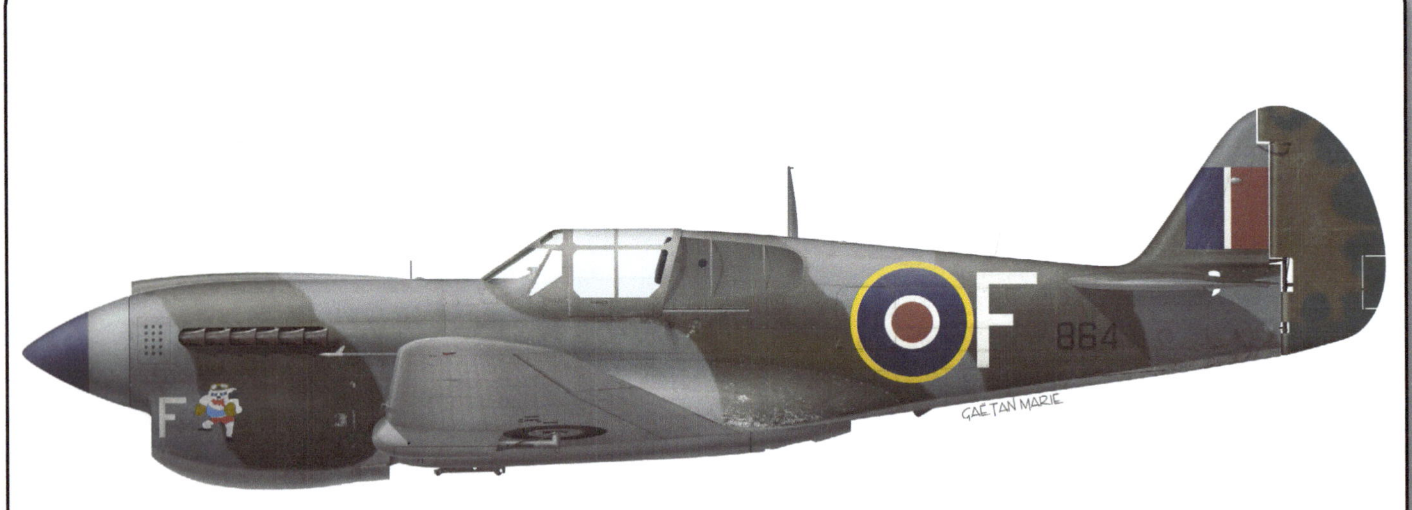

Curtiss Kittyhawk Mk IV 864
No. 135 Squadron, RCAF
Patricia Bay, British Columbia (Canada), summer 1945

Date	Pilot	S/N	Origin	Serial	Code	Fate
18.08.44	F/O Charles E. **HARVILL**	Can./ J.41798	RCAF	**849**		-
30.06.45	F/O Walter D. **FORD**	Can./ J.43046	RCAF	**872**	S	-

Total: 2

Summary of the aircraft known lost by accident - 135 Squadron, RCAF

Date	Pilot	S/N	Origin	Serial	Code	Fate
19.05.45	P/O Stanley **DIXON**	Can./ J.49666	RCAF	**846**	B	-
24.05.45	F/O Thomas **CORNIE**	Can./ J.39535	RCAF	**861**		†
24.07.45	F/L Paul L. **GIBBS**	Can./ J.15108	RCAF	**848**	P	-

Total: 3

No. 135 Squadron's Kittyhawk IVs in March 1945. Visible are 862/C and 858/J above and, below, 847/B, 866/R (with a serial uncommonly painted in white) and 857/V.

<u>**No. 163 Squadron**</u>

This squadron was formed as an Army co-operation unit at Sea Island (Vancouver) in March 1943. Its initial equipment consisted of Bristol Bolingbrokes and North American Harvards. In June, it converted to Hurricanes and changed to the fighter role when Curtiss Kittyhawks were received on 14 October; the new aircraft were transferred from both Nos. 111 and 118 Squadrons on their departure for Europe. At that time, 163 was commanded by S/L JT Wilson. Some Kittyhawks (729, 1057, 1095 and 1098) had a short stay with the squadron as they were transferred to Patricia Bay within a couple of days; new Kittyhawk Mk.IVs (861, 862, 863 and 864) were received in exchange. The fleet now comprised those four and 832, 835, 840, 845, 866, 867, 868, 1029, 1031 and 1040, the last three being Kittyhawk Is while the others were Mk.IVs. In November, the squadron became a full Kittyhawk unit when the last Hurricanes left. A new CO, S/L DL Ramsay, took over on 13 November, but little flying (less than 80 hours in training) was done that month; this figure increased to over 130 in December. In January, the hours almost tripled but no operational flights were carried out and the situation remained unchanged in February, but 163 lost one pilot posted, P/O W Szportan, posted missing on the 5th after he lost control in cloud during a formation practice flight. On 1 March, the first major Kittyhawk accident occurred when P/O ME Myles was unable to lower his undercarriage and was forced to make a belly landing on the grass strip parallel to the runway. Myles was uninjured and 1040 not seriously damaged. A few days later, on the 6th, the RCAF decided to disband the unit to reduce requirements on Western Command and orders were given to 163 to cease operational activity, something it had yet to do anyway. Two days week later, S/L Ramsay was posted to Western Air Command HQ at Vancouver and relinquished command to his A Flight CO, F/L Dennis WP Connolly, whose task was to manage the disbandment that became effective on 15 March 1944. Most of the personnel were posted to No. 32 OTU and No. 133 Squadron. The Kittyhawks were ferried to Patricia Bay on 11 March (729, 731, 832, 838, 840, 845, 1029, 1031, 1035, 1041, 1044, 1058 and 1098), while 836, which could not make the trip that day, was ferried on the 14th.

Summary of the aircraft known lost by accident - 163 Squadron, RCAF

Date	Pilot	S/N	Origin	Serial	Code	Fate
05.02.45	P/O Walter **Szportan**	Can./ J.38039	RCAF	**835**		†

Total: 1

No. 5 Operational Training Unit (OTU)

Formed at Boundary Bay in British Columbia in April 1944 to train crews on Liberator heavy bombers, No. 5 OTU received some Kittyhawks to carry out fighter affiliation sorties. Eight were taken on charge in July, but they were a tiny part of the unit's fleet, the OTU having no less than 37 Mitchells, 36 Liberators and five Bolingbrokes on hand at the time. The Kittyhawks increased to 12 in December, flying an average of 100 hours each month and doubling that effort by the summer of 1945. A deadly accident occurred on 1 November 1944 when, during fighter affiliation, Kittyhawk 839/N, piloted by F/O JE Thomson, collided with Liberator KG290/J. Part of the Kittyhawk's wing was broken off and the aircraft crashed in the bay near White Rock while the Liberator returned to base. With the end of the war in the Far East, activity considerably reduced from 15 August. The Kittyhawks known to have been used by the OTU were 831, 832, 837, 838, 839, 840, 841, 844, 845, 867, 869, 870, 877 and 878.

Summary of the aircraft known lost by accident - 5 OTU, RCAF

Date	Pilot	S/N	Origin	Serial	Code	Fate
05.02.45	F/O John E. **Thomson**	Can./ J.18637	RCAF	**839**	N	†

Total: 1

Kittyhawk 867/PN of No. 5 OTU. The OTU's Kittyhawk squadron used the unit code letter 'P' and an individual aircraft letter.

THE REGISTER

Serial	TOC	Formerly	Type	SOC	Known assignment
720	10.04.42	ET845	Mk.IA	**16.12.46**	132, 133
721	10.04.42	ET847	Mk.IA	10.04.44	132
722	10.04.42	ET849	Mk.IA	09.02.43	132
723	10.0442	ET850	Mk.IA	**23.08.46**	132
724	10.04.42	ET852	Mk.IA	08.09.42	132
725	10.04.42	ET854	Mk.IA	06.10.42	132
726	10.04.42	ET856	Mk.IA	28.02.45	132, 133
727	10.04.42	ET858	Mk.IA	**23.08.46**	132
728	10.04.42	ET860	Mk.IA	09.10.42	132
729	10.04.42	ET862	Mk.IA	**23.08.46**	111, 133
730	10.04.42	ET863	Mk.IA	03.09.42	132
731	10.04.42	ET866	Mk.IA	31.08.44	132, 133
831	26.01.43	43-5706	P-40M-5-CU/Mk.III	**23.08.46**	8 OTU, 5 OTU
832	26.01.43	43-5778	P-40M-10-CU/Mk.III	**23.08.46**	118, 133, 5 OTU
833	26.01.43	43-5699	P-40M-5-CU/Mk.III	09.11.43	118, 132
834	26.01.43	43-5691	P-40M-5-CU/Mk.III	**09.03.46**	*Inst. airframe A 289, Apr-43*
835	26.01.43	43-5779	P-40M-5-CU/Mk.III	02.03.44	163
836	29.01.43	43-5794	P-40M-10-CU/Mk.III	26.07.44	118, 163
837	29.01.43	43-5786	P-40M-10-CU/Mk.III	**23.08.46**	118, 132, 5 OTU
838	29.01.43	43-5787	P-40M-10-CU/Mk.III	**23.08.46**	163, 5 OTU
839	29.01.43	43-5698	P-40M-10-CU/Mk.III	20.11.44	132, 5 OTU
840	29.01.43	43-5802	P-40M-10-CU/Mk.III	**23.08.46**	133, 5 OTU
841	29.01.43	43-5811	P-40M-10-CU/Mk.III	**23.08.46**	5 OTU
842	29.01.43	43-5803	P-40M-10-CU/Mk.III	06.01.44	132
843	03.02.43	43-5812	P-40M-10-CU/Mk.III	26.07.44	132
844	04.02.43	43-5810	P-40M-10-CU/Mk.III	**23.08.46**	5 OTU
845	05.02.43	43-5795	P-40M-10-CU/Mk.III	**23.08.46**	118, 163, 133, 5 OTU
846	06.05.43	42-102568	P-40N-1-CU/Mk.IV	07.07.45	135
847	06.05.43	42-104608	P-40N-1-CU/Mk.IV	**23.08.46**	135
848	06.05.43	42-104548	P-40N-1-CU/Mk.IV	31.08.45	135
849	20.05.43	42-104588	P-40N-1-CU/Mk.IV	**16.12.46**	135
850	20.05.43	42-104668	P-40N-1-CU/Mk.IV	**23.08.46**	135
851	21.05.43	42-104748	P-40N-1-CU/Mk.IV	**27.06.47**	-
852	07.06.43	42-104688	P-40N-1-CU/Mk.IV	**16.12.46**	132, 135
853	07.06.43	42-104648	P-40N-1-CU/Mk.IV	**23.08.46**	-
854	07.06.43	42-104508	P-40N-1-CU/Mk.IV	**23.08.46**	135

855	11.06.43	42-104488	P-40N-1-CU/Mk.IV	**16.12.46**	135
856	22.06.43	42-105191	P-40N-5-CU/Mk.IV	**23.08.46**	135
857	22.06.43	42-105181	P-40N-5-CU/Mk.IV	**23.08.46**	135
858	22.06.43	42-105192	P-40N-5-CU/Mk.IV	**23.08.46**	133, 135
859	07.07.43	42-105179	P-40N-5-CU/Mk.IV	**23.08.46**	135
860	15.07.43	42-105180	P-40N-5-CU/Mk.IV	**23.08.46**	135
861	17.09.43	42-105839	P-40N-5-CU/Mk.IV	21.08.45	135
862	17.09.43	42-105840	P-40N-5-CU/Mk.IV	23.08.45	111, 135
863	17.09.43	42-105842	P-40N-5-CU/Mk.IV	28.09.44	133
864	17.09.43	42-105844	P-40N-5-CU/Mk.IV	**23.08.46**	133
865	17.09.43	42-105846	P-40N-5-CU/Mk.IV	**23.08.46**	130, 135
866	17.09.43	42-105865	P-40N-5-CU/Mk.IV	**23.08.46**	133, 135
867	17.09.43	42-105867	P-40N-5-CU/Mk.IV	**23.08.46**	130, 135, 5 OTU
868	17.09.43	42-105869	P-40N-5-CU/Mk.IV	**23.08.46**	-
869	17.09.43	42-105871	P-40N-5-CU/Mk.IV	**23.08.46**	5 OTU
870	17.09.43	42-105878	P-40N-5-CU/Mk.IV	**23.08.46**	111, 132, 5 OTU
871	19.10.43	43-22888	P-40N-20-CU/Mk.IV	**16.12.46**	135
872	19.10.43	42-106387	P-40N-15-CU/Mk.IV	**21.09.45**	135
873	19.10.43	43-22885	P-40N-20-CU/Mk.IV	**23.08.46**	135
874	19.10.43	43-22882	P-40N-20-CU/Mk.IV	**16.12.46**	135
875	11.01.44	43-23496	P-40N-20-CU/Mk.IV	**23.08.46**	111, 135
876	11.01.44	43-23490	P-40N-20-CU/Mk.IV	18.06.45	133
877	27.01.44	43-23484	P-40N-20-CU/Mk.IV	**23.08.46**	5 OTU
878	31.01.44	43-23487	P-40N-20-CU/Mk.IV	**23.08.46**	5 OTU
879	16.03.44	43-23493	P-40N-20-CU/Mk.IV	**16.12.46**	135
880	11.09.44	42-106396	P-40N-15-CU/Mk.IV	**23.08.46**	135
1028	09.10.41	AK752	Mk.I	**16.08.46**	132, 133
1029	09.10.41	AK773	Mk.I	**23.08.46**	118, 163, 133
1030	14.10.41	AK779	Mk.I	11.12.42	-
1031	14.10.41	AK785	Mk.I	27.10.44	163, 133
1032	16.10.41	AK791	Mk.I	05.05.42	118
1033	17.10.41	AK797	Mk.I	10.06.43	118
1034	16.10.41	AK803	Mk.I	**23.08.46**	118, 133
1035	17.10.41	AK809	Mk.I	**16.08.46**	118, 133
1036	22.10.41	AK815	Mk.I	**02.04.48**	118, 132
1037	22.10.41	AK821	Mk.I	26.04.43	118
1038	22.10.41	AK827	Mk.I	**23.08.46**	118, 133, 132
1039	22.10.41	AK833	Mk.I	22.11.44	14, 133
1040	23.10.41	AK839	Mk.I	28.10.44	163, 133
1041	22.10.41	AK845	Mk.I	**16.08.46**	118, 133
1042	25.10.41	AK851	Mk.I	08.12.43	118, 132
1043	25.10.41	AK857	Mk.I	**16.08.46**	118, 133
1044	03.11.41	AK863	Mk.I	**16.08.46**	111, 163, 133
1045	02.02.42	AK865	Mk.I	**05.03.48**	130, 133
1046	03.11.41	AK869	Mk.I	18.05.43	111
1047	03.11.41	AK875	Mk.I	**23.08.46**	111, 133
1048	03.11.41	AK881	Mk.I	08.08.42	111
1049	06.11.41	AK887	Mk.I	19.03.42	111
1050	06.11.41	AK893	Mk.I	**16.12.46**	111, 14, 133
1051	06.11.41	AK899	Mk.I	**23.08.46**	111
1052	06.11.41	AK905	Mk.I	**16.08.46**	111, 133
1053	06.11.41	AK911	Mk.I	04.05.45	111, 14, 132, 133
1054	02.02.42	AK914	Mk.I	20.08.43	130, 14
1055	02.02.42	AK915	Mk.I	27.08.42	130
1056	02.02.42	AK930	Mk.I	29.05.43	130
1057	02.02.42	AK933	Mk.I	**16.08.46**	130, 133
1058	06.11.41	AK940	Mk.I	**16.08.46**	111, 133
1059	28.01.42	AK950	Mk.I	02.08.43	14, 132
1060	28.01.42	AK952	Mk.I	08.10.42	14
1061	20.11.42	AK954	Mk.I	10.12.42	111
1062	20.11.42	AK968	Mk.I	22.09.44	132
1063	28.01.42	AK978	Mk.I	**23.08.46**	14
1064	23.04.42	AK979	Mk.I	**23.08.46**	132
1065	20.11.41	AK982	Mk.I	08.12.43	111, 14
1066	28.01.42	AK983	Mk.I	**16.08.46**	14, 132, 111, 133

1067	28.01.42	AK986	Mk.I	**23.08.46**	14,133
1069	28.01.42	AK987	Mk.I	**23.08.46**	14, 133
1069	28.01.42	AK989	Mk.I	18.05.43	14, 111
1070	01.12.41	AK996	Mk.I	10.12.42	111
1071	28.01.42	AL109	Mk.I	25.07.44	14, 111
1072	01.12.41	AL110	Mk.I	**30.03.46**	14, 111
1073	28.01.42	AL113	Mk.I	**23.08.46**	14
1074	23.04.42	AL115	Mk.I	**16.08.46**	132, 133
1075	03.12.41	AL124	Mk.I	**23.08.46**	111, 14
1076	23.03.42	AL135	Mk.I	**23.08.46**	132
1077	02.02.42	AL136	Mk.I	12.03.43	130
1078	02.02.42	AL137	Mk.I	**23.08.46**	133
1079	10.12.41	AL138	Mk.I	10.12.42	111
1080	28.01.42	AL144	Mk.I	29.02.44	14, 111
1081	02.02.42	AL150	Mk.I	29.02.44	132
1082	03.12.41	AL152	Mk.I	**23.08.46**	118
1083	13.12.41	AL166	Mk.I	10.12.42	14, 111
1084	02.02.42	AL171	Mk.I	**16.08.46**	133
1085	13.12.41	AL180	Mk.I	05.03.42	111
1086	23.03.42	AL191	Mk.I	**22.10.53**	14, 132, 133
1087	16.12.41	AL194	Mk.I	13.06.44	111, 133
1088	02.02.42	AL201	Mk.I	10.12.42	14, 111
1089	13.01.42	AL210	Mk.I	08.12.42	118
1090	13.12.41	AL212	Mk.I	16.05.42	111
1091	13.12.41	AL214	Mk.I	**23.08.46**	111
1092	13.12.41	AL216	Mk.I	09.10.42	118, 132
1093	13.12.41	AL218	Mk.I	23.12.43	111, 14
1094	13.01.42	AL220	Mk.I	11.12.42	118
1095	13.12.41	AL222	Mk.I	**23.08.46**	118
1096	13.01.42	AL224	Mk.I	26.07.44	133
1097	13.01.42	AL226	Mk.I	10.06.43	118
1098	13.01.42	AL227	Mk.I	**16.08.46**	118, 111
1099	13.01.42	AL228	Mk.I	23.12.43	14

In red, serial not used, aircraft written-off before the RCAF sequence number was adopted.

Kittyhawk AK752, the first Kittyhawk issued to the RCAF, taken shortly after its arrival in the country in October 1941.

SQUADRONS! - The series

Donald James Matthew BLAKESLEE DFC

Supermarine Spitfire Mk.VB EN951
No. 133 (Eagle) Squadron
Flight Lieutenant D. J. M. Blakeslee
CAN./ J.4551
Gravesend (UK), August 1942

Charles Cuthbertson LEARMONTH DFC*

Douglas Boston Mk. III A28-9 (ex-AL891)
No. 22 Squadron RAAF
Squadron Leader C. C. Learmonth
Aus. 385
Port Moresby (New Guinea), spring 1943

Hans Anton MAURENBRECHER

Curtiss P-40N-35-CU C3-560
No. 120 (NEI) Squadron
Major H. Maurenbrecher
Biak (New Guinea), 1943-1946

Roland Prosper BEAMONT DSO* DFC*

Hawker Tempest Mk V JN751
No. 150 Wing
Wing Commander R. P. Beamont
RAF No. 41849
Bradwell Bay (UK), April 1944

Ronald Thomas SUSANS DSO DFC

North American P-51D-25-NT A68-724
No. 77 Squadron, RAAF
Squadron Leader R. T. Susans
O.4391
Bofu (Japan), 1947

James Henry LACEY DFM*

Supermarine Spitfire Mk.XIV RN135
No. 17 Squadron
Squadron Leader J. H. Lacey
RAF No. 112709
Seletar (Singapore), autumn 1945

Introducing's RAF In Combat and Bravo Bravo Aviation's collection of highly-detailed and historically accurate, high-quality aviation prints.
For more information on available prints, please visit :

or

Prints in connection with the book:

PL-262: BR Walker
PL-263: AD Nesbitt
PL-264: KA Boomer
PL-265: AM Yuile
PL-266: IC Ormston
PL-267: JE Sheppard

www.ingramcontent.com/pod-product-compliance
Lightning Source LLC
LaVergne TN
LVHW071647180726
843512LV00002B/405